SIMON PHILIP

IAN SMITH

WANNA SEE A PENGUIN?

OXFORD
UNIVERSITY PRESS

Hey. Wanna see a penguin?

You betcha!
But where?

Don't you worry.
I know *just* the place.
Come with me.

You don't have to be a penguin expert like me
to spot one. It's pretty easy when you
know what to look for.

They're **black and white,**

distinctive . . .

And look—**there's one now!**

What?!

Penguins don't have stripes.

I know.

I was just testing.

Well done.

Come on.
This way . . .

Penguins come in all shapes and sizes,
but have many common features.

They're black and white,

distinctive,
don't have stripes . . .

And look!

There's another one!

Gosh. I'm not sure what *that* is,
but it's *definitely* **NOT** a penguin!

And anyway,
penguins can swim.

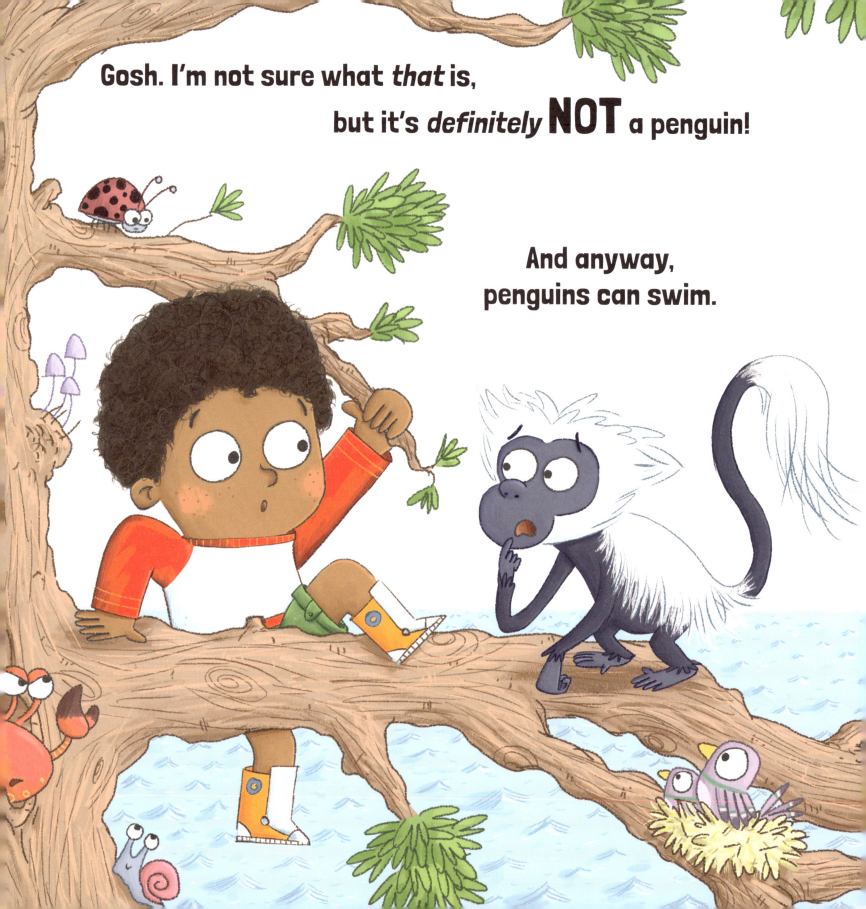

Not many people know that.
But you're right. There's no
catching you out!

Now, look!

Over
there . . .

Don't be silly!
Penguins have *legs.*

I *know*.

You're looking in
the wrong place.

I meant over **there!**

Oh, come on.

Penguins don't have **horns!** Or **hooves!**

Really? A dog?!
But penguins have **webbed** feet!

Goodness, you are demanding.

Alright, I'll show you an *actual* penguin.
Follow me.

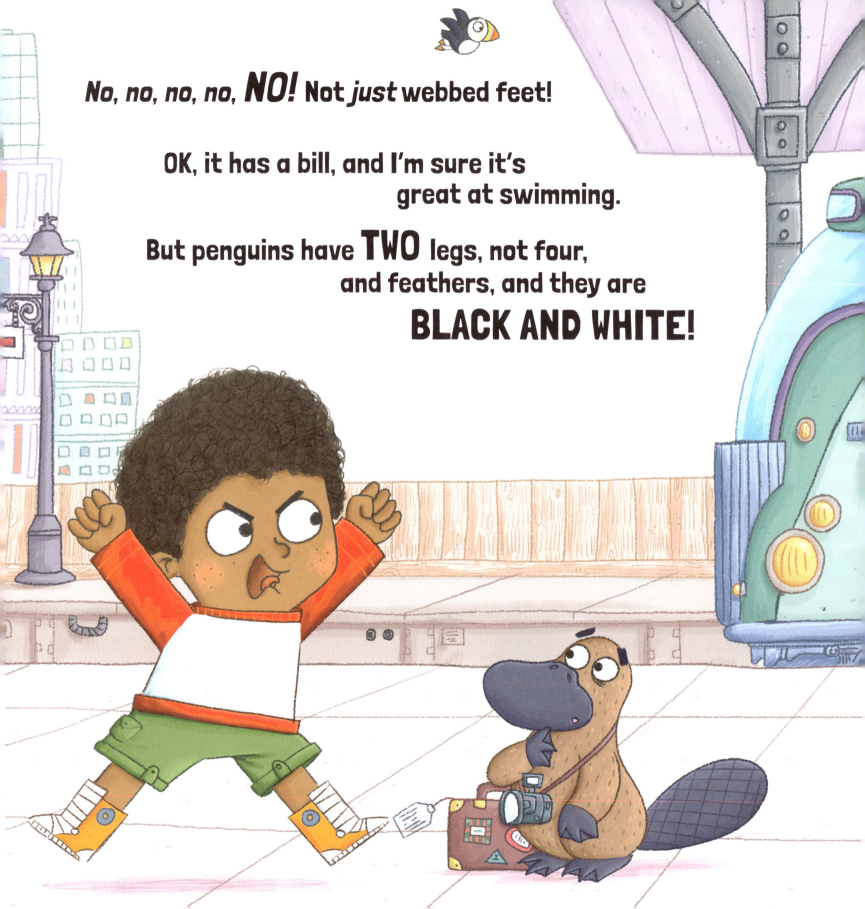

No, no, no, no, **NO!** Not *just* webbed feet!

OK, it has a bill, and I'm sure it's great at swimming.

But penguins have **TWO** legs, not four, and feathers, and they are

BLACK AND WHITE!

Right, well if you want to see *that* sort of penguin, *that's* what I'll show you!

There.
Happy now?

No! That's a puffin!
Puffins *fly*.
Penguins *don't*.

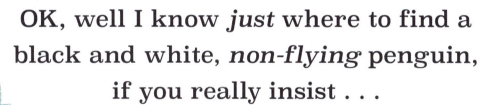

OK, well I know *just* where to find a
black and white, *non-flying* penguin,
if you really insist . . .

Huh? A panda?!

Pandas can't fly.

True—*but you're forgetting all the other things!*

Oh.

Yes, I . . . well . . .
ummm . . .
it depends how you—

Be honest.

No. No, I'm not.
But I *really* want to see one,
and I thought if we looked together,
you might be able to help me.
I'm sorry.

That's ok. I understand.
I'd like to see one too. But there aren't
any penguins around here. Sorry.

Wanna see a . . .

Zebra

Scientists aren't really sure why zebras have stripes. One idea is that they may help zebras to recognise one another: each zebra's stripes are unique!

Puffin

A puffin's bill changes colour during the year, transforming from dull grey in the winter to an outrageous orange in spring!

Duck-billed Platypus

They may look cute, but male duck-billed platypuses are actually venomous! They can use sharp spikes on their heels to sting other animals. Maybe that's why platypuses spend most of their time alone . . .

Panda

You'll like this fact: pandas sometimes do handstands when they wee! This helps them leave their scent higher up a tree. Probably best you don't try this at home . . .

Colobus Monkey

Native to central Africa, these monkeys spend almost all their time up in the trees. They are brilliant at jumping from tree to tree and even use branches as trampolines!

Orca

Orcas can weigh up to 6 tons–that's the same as about 600 watermelons! They can swim at speeds of up to 54 kilometres per hour, which is much faster than even the speediest watermelon.

Valais Blackneck Goat

These goats have strong legs which are ideal for climbing and walking long distances. Like all goats, they look absolutely nothing like penguins.

Dalmatian

Although known for their spotted coats, Dalmatians are born completely white! Even once their spots appear (when they're around four weeks old), each Dalmatian's pattern is unique!

OXFORD
UNIVERSITY PRESS

Great Clarendon Street, Oxford OX2 6DP

Oxford University Press is a department of the University of Oxford.
It furthers the University's objective of excellence in research, scholarship,
and education by publishing worldwide. Oxford is a registered trade mark of
Oxford University Press in the UK and in certain other countries

Text © Simon Philip 2023
Illustration © Ian Smith 2023

The moral rights of the author and artist have been asserted

Database right Oxford University Press (maker)

First published 2023

British Library Cataloguing in Publication Data available

ISBN: 978-0-19-278356-1

1 3 5 7 9 10 8 6 4 2

Printed in China

Paper used in the production of this book is a natural,
recyclable product made from wood grown in sustainable forests.
The manufacturing process conforms to the environmental
regulations of the country of origin